T0381366

FARPOINT MINDSTATION II

THE QUEST FOR PURPOSE

BY

DR. DAVID R. HUFF

 www.trafford.com

North America & international
toll-free: 1 888 232 4444 (USA & Canada)
fax: 812 355 4082

DEDICATION

THIS BOOK IS DEDICATED TO DR. ERICA BERNER
FRIEND, COLLEAGUE, AND CAT FANCIER

CONTENTS

FORWARD

Farpoint Mindstation II contains many poems written in the Terzanelle poetry form. The Terzanelle form first appeared in 1969, it is a combination of the Villanelle and the Terza Rima poetry forms. The Terzanelle uses the interlocked rhyme of a Terza Rima, but in the Villanelle's form of five triplets and a quatrain.

Included are some of the classics from Farpoint Mindstation I. The poem **Allegiances**, which won a prize at the 2006 International Poet's Society Convention, maybe found in this volume.

The Tea Maker Of Hail, Saudi Arabia

THE TERZANELLE'S FORM:

Stanza 1	first a
	first b
	second a
Stanza 2	second b
	first c
	repeat first b
Stanza 3	second c
	first d
	repeat first c
Stanza 4	second d
	first e
	repeat first d
Stanza 5	second e
	first f
	repeat first e
Stanza 6	second f
	repeat first a
	repeat first f
	repeat second a

A WASTED LIFE

The yellow star slowly emerges above the mound of vanity
Fetid vapors of forgotten objects assault the nose
Existing in the rotting world, shadows of small humanity

Waste foragers consigned to relieving family woes
All live for the next treasure truck to belch its collection
Fetid vapors of forgotten objects assault the nose

For the throw away waifs fragile life has no protection
Cans and broken fetishes are the only objects of value
All live for the next treasure truck to belch its collection

The material jungle drones on without the slightest clue
Castoff luxuries all stored in lines of plastic barrels
Cans and broken fetishes are the only objects of value

None notice when a child dies among the mound's perils
A life of lost value destined to find others waste
Castoff luxuries all stored in lines of plastic barrels

It is time for the truth to be faced
The yellow star slowly emerges above the mound of vanity
A life of lost value destined to find other's waste
Existing in the rotting world, shadows of small humanity.

Palestinian Boy In A Garbage Dump

ALLEGIANCE

I pledge allegiance to the credit cards
And the debt for which they stand
One uncertainty about my nation
Under a politically correct deity
With limited liberty, sometimes justice, and not for all

I pledge allegiance to a gas guzzling car
And the knowledge it will not travel far
One big insurance bill
Under a pile of unpaid bills
With limited happiness, sometimes anger, and no relief at all

I pledge allegiance to political correctness
And to the conformity for which it stands
One view subject to change at any time
Under pressure at work
With limited thought, sometimes confusion, and no sense at all

"All in all, just another brick in the wall"

Food Offering To A Queen Of Egypt

AUTHOR'S COMMENT

The next three poems are a cycle trilogy. They were written in Saudi Arabia and are about the Final Exams at Prince Mohamed University (PMU).

The first poem is about the time period preceding Final exam week. The second poem takes place during the final exams. The third is about the time after the finals are finished and grading is in progress.

Two of the three poems are written in the Terzanelle form. The poems are based on true events.

BRAINSTORM RISING

In the baking Eastern Province a time for change nears
The last days slowly quicken their pace of passing
Gathering paper clouds are understood by the unlearned peers

Storm Masters stealthily gather fuel for the coming massing
Places and times are selected to invigilate for survivors
The last days slowly quicken their pace of passing

Clever pit falls and snares hidden to catch evading connivers
The building ozone of uncertain anticipation alert the wary
Places and times are selected to invigilate for survivors

The low mark ones whisper desperate words of how long to terry
The prepared ones are ready to weather the storm in good form
The building ozone of uncertain anticipation alert the wary

The brainstorm will arrive when fear has become the norm
Pencils and paper wielded by determined minds prepare for battle
The prepared ones are ready to weather the storm in good form

Winds of certainty blow away the idle gossip and wasted prattle
In the baking Eastern Province a time for change nears
Pencils wielded by determined minds prepare for battle
Gathering paper clouds are understood by the unlearned peers

FINAL EXAM

Dedicated to: Dr. Robin Bodkin

The moment finally arrives
The time of books, notes, and late nights ends
Trial by pencil and the nemesis clock as reality bends
Myriads of bold interrogations bombard as the mind contrives
Memory and clever tactics battle for every mark

Confidence flags as the vision of facts goes dark
With each passing test page the doubt imp works its misery
Time escapes the mind's grasp as if by sorcery
In the last moments of the battle reality becomes cold and start

On the call to halt the test ogres extinguish the last spark
In the end, only the final mark gives or deprives.

AFTERMATH

Dedicated to: Dean Robin Starke

The fall mind-quake passes through silent halls
Survivors wonder about, seeking clues to who came through
A learned band swims the paper sea to make their final call

Few know who will end up in the cruel failure stew
Machines and red pens move swiftly deciding many fates
Survivors wonder about, seeking clues to who came through

The learned ones barely notice an aftershock of class rates
Soon a gathering will assemble to judge people and events
Machines and red pens move swiftly deciding many fates

Forms and e-mail flotsam washing over desks, many angry vents
Who among the many will be worthy to join the Core Crew?
Soon a gathering will assemble to judge people and events

As the paper storm abates, all that remains is the shrew
At the Keep of Knowledge, trial by finals fades as a mirage
Who among the many are worthy to join the Core Crew?

Posted marks reveal to all the pain and joy montage
The fall mind-quake passes through silent halls
At the Keep of Knowledge, trial by finals fades as a mirage
A learned band swims the paper sea to make their final call.

CHARGE OF THE LIGHT SHABOBS

The brainstorm has passed, some smile, others aghast
The mark javelins are hurled to find their targets
For the prepared and agile the javelin sails harmlessly past

Dull wits and inattention earn a painful strike without regrets
Wounded pride and an uncertain future, the Shabobs cannot go
The mark javelins are hurled to find their targets

Many stories and desperate wasta plots are carefully made so
A gathering of the Pleading Council is quickly prepared for
Wounded pride and an uncertain future, the Shabobs cannot go

Last chance for the learning wounded to find a way into the Core
Allied with parents, the charge of the Shabobs readies
A gathering of the Pleading Council is quickly prepared for

Learned ones carefully positioned with facts calmly steadies
The unknowing ones have dreadfully made their final blunder
Allied with parents, the charge of the Shabobs readies

Accurate records and attendance sheets volley and tear asunder
The brainstorm has passed, some smile, others aghast
The unknowing ones have dreadfully made their final blunder
For the prepared and agile the javelin sails harmlessly past.

The Charge of the Shabobs

INTO THE HANDS OF FAITH

Dedicated to: The Myanmar Monks

Ancient shining spires testifying to knowledge and defiance
In a land of Red and Green Taos
A people little in need of foreign science

The green mailed fist demands from all obedient kowtows
Grim green phalanxes parade about with death on their minds
In a land of Red and Green Taos

The Red robes chant their wisdom where knowledge shines
Patience with open hearts and hands greet the people
Grim green phalanxes parade about with death on their minds

Green Tyrants disdainfully ignore the fearful harmless sheeple
Without force chanted words only fall upon impotent ears
Patience with open hearts and hands greet the people

An endless line of resolute truth marches onward amid cheers
The Green Soldiers can't stop faith or ideas from growing
Without force chanted words only fall upon impotent ears

The Red Monks walk into the hands of faith chanting peace
Ancient shining spires testifying to knowledge and defiance
The Green Soldiers can't stop faith or ideas from growing
A people little in need of foreign science.

The Peace Walkers

In Memory

In everyone's life there is a favorite relative. It is a sad moment when they pass away. I was fortunate two have two favorite relatives, Aunt Sara and Uncle Andy. I was asked to write a poem for each of their funeral services and read them as a part of the eulogy. It was an honor to perform both tasks. The next two poems are theirs and are now a part of the family's history.

AND ONE RETURNED

Dedicated to: Uncle Andy

Gray skies at the Arc of Remembrance greet the tribe

Walls lined with names of the past seeking to remain in the present

A pure white piece of fire rock marks the last of the departed spirit

Green lined thrones for the grieved one and the tribe elders

Sacred music plays as the silent mass assembles

Time to speak words of a life past that some remember well

Ponder the readings from the Biblical tome, how much will hit home?

A final declaration is intoned to the beloved's ashes

Little to lose nothing to gain, gone now the tears and the pain

The cycle of the mortal is complete, renewal time is at hand

A final act of faith, the release of the winged free spirits

Upon the opening of the basket, all fly away to meet destiny

All, except one noticed by few, the one who returned

Low to the earth with frequent stops the One returns to the Arc

Among the slowly departing tribe the grieving chieftain seeks solstice

The winged spirit lingers unseen for a moment and silently disappears

The returned One's mission is complete, soon they will be meet again

RETURN OF THE CHIEFTAIN

In Memory Of Aunt Sara

Truly as the Returned One came back to the Memorial Place
Time has now arrived for the separated ones to reunite
Life never ceases, it goes on in a more perfect way
Remember their names, for they are a part of you always
A time of tears has passed, recall them kindly with a smile

His Life Journey is worthy of daily remembrances by many
A destination passes from thought as a cloud on a windy day
A Chieftain's zen; Honored Father, warrior, and loyal mate
A Worthy man deserving of respect, admiration, and memory
Peace and happiness are now the companions of the Chieftain

A chapter now ends, but the book continues to be written
What then must we do?
Honor the return of the Chieftain as he gave honor to your lives

AUTHOR'S COMMENTS

The next three poems tell of a trip to Las Vegas, NV. The 2006 ISP poetry convention provided the reason for the trip

<u>Colorful Personality</u> is about airport security and its necessary aggravations. <u>Burnt Bag Blues</u> tells a true story about what happened to my baggage upon arrival in Las Vegas. <u>Gomorran Love Song</u> tells of a journey through a gambling casino. The Gomorran Women are symbols for the many slot machines found in the casino.

COLORFUL PERSONALITY

Green are we, to no one do we give any harm
The cyber-gov declares we are as clean as a white glove
Trust us in secure places and you will never hear an alarm
A tidy tribe are we, approved of by the poli-parrots above
How does one become a green remains to be seen!

Yellow is an odd fellow, different and likes to bellow
Such a politically incorrect rascal with a wrong lean, a fiend!
Who could be so unmello, perhaps a writer or a player of a cello?
Screen them twice, check the socks, they may not be clean
So easy to be a yellow fellow, just look mean

Red, the color of dread and the innocent dead
Cloaked Hunwoolies seeking the hidden moment to rampage
Vile scenes created by those of means, lost in madness in the head
Speaking an unpopular thought in this age will land you in a cage!
The false one, most often with a gun, a rue soul in a coat of green

Standing in a line all safe with a color by your name
Around you is a chameleon, a viper, and a poet playing a head game!

Colorful Person

BURNT BAG BLUES

Early morning trekking time
Time to go to West Gomorrah Town
Bag packed with clothes all pressed and fine
Air Tramp ticket in hand, no reason to feel down
Little touch of Scare-port security, just stand in line

Lurking in the underworld of Hot-lanta, a vile joker
Beware of the Bag Clown, the grand trickster of dismay
No one ever sees this nasty bag croaker
Even a camera cannot deter the Clown's nefarious play
On a brazen caper, a bag is turned into a melted smoker

Char black melted gaping hole greets my paralyzed eyes
This vacation killer cannot be anything I would ever own!
No one answers my desperate quietly whispered whys
All my fun and dreams parade before me, scorched and blown
Hit by the Clown's most hideous and ruinous pies

When you next go a flying
Avoid Air Tramp where the Bag Clown is suitcase frying.

GOMORRAN LOVE SONG

Humanity staring transfixed upon banks of blinking lights
The one armed women tirelessly ply their trade
Sacrifices of hard earned treasure disappear along with hope
All about, but not nearby, the allusive siren sings
Perhaps a generous gift will induce a lady of chance to sing

In an eye blink despair turns into ersatz ecstasy
She appears without warning with a burst of flashing lights
A dissonant raw primitive fanfare falls upon eager ears
Magically a treasure trove of gift coins appear in her lap
A reward stolen from the willing and unwitting

False bravery urges the wealth seeker further down the path
The song continues until the last funds evaporate
Only the silent money understands the Gomorran love song
The mirage of a life of ease dances to the alluring song
Humanity stares transfixed at their empty bags of treasure

Only the one armed women win in Gomorrah.

Gormoran One Armed Woman

AUTHOR'S COMMENTS

The first year I spent in the KSA was in the N.W. province of Hail, which is also the name of the main city. The University of Hail (a.k.a Hell U) and the time spent in the area was a major eye opening experience. It was here I learned the true meaning of the phrase, "Adapt, Improvise, and Overcome." The Mishar Dryer is testimony to this credo. The next five poems were written while at Hail.

What Happens When A Camel Sees Its Shadow?

DAY OF THE DUNES

Sparkling flowing crystalline sea beyond the eyes' reach
Days of brain frying heat with nights of bone cracking chills
Meaningless time flows together with the ever shifting rills
Unseen life leaves marks in the sand giving lessons to teach
Where gold is worthless, water is the currency of life

Eternally blowing winds laden with sand cutting like a knife
Bedu living in unity with the changing dunes
Citizens of the dunes, from their tents come the old tunes
Wonderers of the perilous lands living a peaceful life
Life on the orange dry sea obeys only one rule, survival!

The constant rhythm of the sands ignores the sun's arrival
Beauty and danger beyond any man-animal's gift of speech.

The Al-Nufud Desert Sand Dunes

DESERT VIXEN

In the land of pious Arabs a breeze of discontent blows
From the lower African land of Mandela she came
Dressing in black and hiding behind a veil isn't her game
Fried goat with rice never passes by her modern tuned nose
Woe to the poor fool who tries to put this one in a cage

Worldly sages avoid the vixen on a temperamental rampage
Young and liberated in an ancient land of tradition and law
Coy words with flashes of flesh, the Vixen's shock and awe
Compromises grudgingly must be made to earn a fine wage
In the desert land the Vixen seeks the mirage of peace

Change and tradition must reconcile for the turmoil to cease
By the light of a full desert moon a Vixen bays its woes.

The Desert Vixen

Note From Hail

Imagine a place in Araby land
Sitting among elderly peaks
A place where little gets out of hand
Five times a day the mosque speaks
Four black ribbons wind through the high cold sand

Imagine a place, women go unseen except for their eyes and beaks
Sitting among elegant wealth, the many with little
A place where chilled mountain winds constantly speak
Five times a day all things cease to ponder life's riddle
Four flashing neon lights beckon to passerbys, bargains await

Why only imagine such a place?
Just go to Hail!

AUTHOR'S COMMENT

The next poem, <u>Second Christmas Away</u> is a retro-poem written in Hail, KSA. No one went home for Christmas that year. For me it was a time of remembering when the first Christmas away (Dec. 25, 1973) happened in S.E. Asia. This poem contains a very real undertone of anger.

SECOND CHRISTMAS AWAY

In the dim mists of a long ago seldom remembered time
A day of memories became forfeit to a madness
Youthful ideals are reshaped on the anvil of hate and fear
The day of Peace finds little meaning when life is at stake
The heat of dismay slowly cools into a concealed hatred

The time turtle travels onward towards new todays
The moments of a stranger in Araby land becomes the new now
Ancient ways and voices collide with the unleashed modern mind
Silent reality crystallizes a day of Peace will be forgotten
The thawing of the old hatred slowly continues

For the Vortrekker Christmas 2006 will not be

AUTHOR'S COMMENT

The Saudi Arabian experience has provided both a new perspective of world events and how different the reaction is to a major piece of history. Given the 911 attack, I saw the death by hanging of Iraq's Sadam Hussein as a just event. It shocked me how the Arabs regarded the same event as a time for mourning and anger towards those who committed the deed. After becoming more familiar with both Islam and the Arab culture, I understand the basis for the feelings. However, as an American, I still hold my original opinions.

TYRANT'S END

Death and Fear, the brides of the all powerful
Together they sire the children who devour humanity
All about weak minions reflect the invincible one's vanity
False prosperity displays built on the backs of the sorrowful
The tyrant seeks gifts for his brides, an empire will do

Only a fool dares to drink hate and war's lethal brew
The fog of total power gives the illusion of glorious victory
Conflict draws away life, reality becomes a painful story
With each defeat the Death bride becomes a dreadful shrew
The Fear bride devours the tyrant's soul with vengeful rage

The minions revolt, setting the failed leader's final stage
A death room at twilight hour seals the end lawfully

Author's Comments

Over the last thirty years I have been asked many times, am I a revolutionary? Guess the question arose from my many un-politically correct poems and opinions. After some thought, my answer is; No, I am actually an evolutionary.

Revolution seeks a violent change within a short period of time. Most revolutions fail because no one ever thought about the future beyond the moment of victory.

The evolutionary seeks change over a long period of time by using the tools of persuasion. The political lampoon is one of those tools. Sometimes change can be accomplished by pointing out the problem to the masses.

The following poems are my evolutionary contribution to political incorrectness.

BUREAU-CRITTER

A satire about hurricane relief

Twas a sitting on my porch, my brain about to scorch
Place is a mess, need help I must confess
Saw it coming down the street on pigeon feet
A cross-eyed, flop eared purple paper chucker
Oh lordy, it's heaving a wad of forms straight at me!

Red taped hair, just a clucking without a care
Spitting paper clips and flicking cards from both hips
Heard it say, use a pen of black if you want some jack
Won't touch a drop of gin, but it sure wants my SSN
Oh mercy me, where can all that promised help be?

Full of writer's cramp and my feet are still damp
Forms are filled and gone, but so are the bureau-critters
Watch them going up the street, angry people tired of defeat
They are a hunting the do nothing paper chuckers
Happy day, the purple paper chucker is now at bay!

HOMELAND SOCIAL INSECURITY

Working hard and saluting the flag was an American's bag
All I get now is a hollow clunk and the poli-parrot's hollar
Working sometimes and getting shot at is the latest sorry gag
There was once the ring of the silver dollar

Billions to go whiz on the other guy's campfire
The young go out and come home to a failed promise
Retiring is such peril, the money lost in a stock market pyre
All the poli-hotair makes even a patriot a doubting Thomas

Why should anyone think about it or even care?
It could be you in the alley box we would next give a stare!

HURLY BURLY PLUS ONE

The day of change is now past
"Vox populi" silently waits and watches
Sophomore pundits all aghast

The humbled leader belatedly admits botches
Servants in uniform silently smile
"Vox populi" silently waits and watches

The new power balance goes on trial
How soon can peace be found?
Servants in uniform silently smile

The media magi's idle banters continue to hound
Hot words fade away as the unity breeze cools
How soon can peace be found?

The issues resolved nationwide without war tools
A lesson unlearned by fanatics living by the gun
Hot words fade away as the unity breeze cools

The moment in history when the people won
The day of change is now past
A lesson unlearned by fanatics living by the gun
Sophomore pundits all aghast

ODIOUS DUTY

Sashayed down to the election

Nearly hurled when I saw the selection

Got to sign your name to get into the game

Pencil in hand, marking away with only me to blame

Four more years of another sorry collection.

RUNAWAY BAY: OUT OF MANY ONE

Dedicated to: Aunt June

Under the cloak of deception the Mind Quest comes to Jamaica,

Place of the Rastafar, Bob Marley, magic brownies, and silent truths,

While traveling the countryside I listen to the Many speak,

Silently I watch as they opine and banter about each other,

The driver announces; one off at Runaway Bay, three stops to go,

Must be a Spirit Talker going to Whispering Cave!

No, tis a Marley Mon, wants to hear music and drink Red Stripes,

Ye be all daft, tis a Woman seeking a gree-gree boon!

Might be a Naughty Boy wanting magic brownies to see the pixies,

Driver mon, who is this strange one that goes to Runaway Bay?

Out of many, One, nothing else I know, next stop the knowing moment!

My stop, fine day for a swim at the beach

Peace be with you all!

Ab hoc et ab hac ab illa!

Why assume the worst in others?

CARTOON BY A BABOON

In a tree by the light of a full moon sat a very clever baboon
Through jungle shadows creatures soared, chattered, and roared
With charcoal in paw the monk began to thoughtfully draw

Soon the critters began to lampoon, even a wayward raccoon
Each sketch was gored, an angry mosquito also scored
Red faced and clench jawed, one last try at an idea unflawed

By dawn's first light, in the tree the baboon left its cartoon
All about the jungle snored, even the python looked bored
By noon curiosity gnawed, the animals came and guffawed

All came to see the baboon's large mirror left for you and me
Life can be funny if you decide not to be a hateful dumb bunny!

The Baboon Without His Cartoon

THREE DESIRES

Three desires shared by all, each holding Peace in the balance,

The foundation desire; Freedom from fear, the tearing of the valance,
Fear, the invisible acid corrodes the mind until failure leads,
Fear spawns hate and doubt, the fertile soil of war and vile deeds,

The left supporting desire is tolerance, the fabric of unity,
Tolerance weaves together differences turning them into immunity,
Tolerance clothes harmony and tranquility with the glow of diversity,

The right supporting desire is education, a shield against adversity,
Education is the mind field where the grain of knowledge grows,
Education gives clear vision to see a future that glows,

When the three desires are met, Peace and Prosperity are brothers

SEASONS MERRY DAY GREETINGS

Dedicated to: Political Incorrectness

As easy as a porcupine walking through a balloon store
A time of material madness and religious correctness
Remembering what to say and when is such a chore
Anyone know who started this verbal selectness?
Seems trivial when looking at the nightly news gore

Holy days once very sacred, not a time for the reckless
A time to put away swords and remember how to respect
Each busy moment blinded by the glare of the feckless
Where is peace to be found in a material world so suspect?
All about false pride worn like a cheap necklace

Peace be onto you
It may not be politically correct
At least it is direct
Words you can speak plain and true.

AUTHOR'S COMMENTS

As a disabled retired veteran, I have seen and experienced life in the military and coming home to a hostile nation. It is an easy task to stand for a nation, especially when the nation supported the war, gives a parade,and grand homecoming. The WWII veteran is referred to as a part of the greatest generation. So be it.

The Vietnam war veterans were a part of the most tested and enduring generation in American history. They fought three wars, the shooting war, the war with their own nation; which mistrusted them,and the war within themselves. The last war is still being fought by some vets today.

The Vietnam Veteran's gave their children to another war, Desert Storm. It is a testimony to their loyalty, they once again stood for a nation right or wrong.

The next series of poems are given to the reader with the hope you can feel some of the experience.

The Ebon Wall

ONCE UPON AN EBON WALL

The Genesis Poem! (8/30/88)

Silently I sit looking at the name etched black mirror to the past,

My mind slowly returns to the din and chaotic pall of days lost,

As in all acts of armed insanity, the fallen must be counted!

Among the fallen in each war will be a first and a last,

In a far off jungle bleached bones await their turn,

They too will be an entry on the Ebon Wall!

All about me others bring personal offerings of remembrance,

The remembrances are testimonies to their silent pain,

A few seek a boon from the Ebon named Slabs,

Slowly they rub pencils across thin sheets of paper,

In my head an old song echoes: Little to lose, nothing to gain,

From the center the Dark Edifice rises with many names,

Mercifully with the coming of Peace it tapers to a few,

I stand before the year denoting my time of trial and fear,

I stare mutely at the blank line among the many names,

Someone quite rudely broke their appointment with the Grim Reaper,

Once upon an Ebon Wall, one soul has decided not to heed the call,

Ebon Wall, monument to death and despair, bear witness!

I am alive and live for Peace!

WALL WITNESS

Ict bin ein Berliner
JFK

Since time began to record, walls are built to fall
Even the greatest wall of them all failed to stop change
Walls can neither keep life in nor keep it out no matter how tall
Every time one is built people start acting very strange

A mole's delight digging deep out of the light
Listen carefully for the hairless ones building a stealth road below
Trog-travelers risking all just to be where free speech is a right
Dark silent ones scurrying about listening to wires, none saying hello

Phantom artists with dancing volk play their roles of defiance
With rapier wit they are pit alone and unarmed to shame the wall
Each day confident self-reliance meets sharp wire and cold stone
From within the cracks form and spread until the fall

"Let them hate, so long as they fear", so said a Roman Emperor
Fear us as our hate crushes your wall, reply the People!

Special note

This poem is about the Berlin Wall. Written in 1990, the poem celebrates
the fall of the Wall signaling the end of the Cold War.

The Berlin Wall 1990

MEMORY DAY

Dedicated to: The Veterans

365 since you last pondered who died and who survived,

Every war has a first and last to fall or return,

War always has a first, but never is the last,

Gardens of Stone grow larger each season with guardians of freedom,

Solemn survivors give rituals of respect, quietly they envy the dead,

Fallen ones are at Peace for they no longer remember the horrors,

Mourn for the living for each day is Memory Day of a season in hell,

Quo fas, gloria, et pax ducunt

TEARS IN THE RAIN

Monsoon rains pour down as I go about my duties,

Forgetting the soaked body, the Mind ponders how it arrived here,

The Soul silently looks on wondering will the rain wash away the war,

In a sea of raw emotion the Spirit steers clear of despair's shoals,

About me in the steady deluge all resolutely perform as one,

Our tears are washed away in the rain, unknowing of each's pain.

MOMENTS LOST IN TIME

Memorial Day 2006
"Long live the fighters"

A tiding of hope and fear to cheer on the new war fighters
The communal shards of shared reality know it is time
The command voices ring out, the sands of mars beckon
A fragile shard shatters into two pieces, two stories begin

A mecha-banshee bird awaits at the ready with its open maw
Silently the warriors bravely enter with their shattered shards
Somber on-lookers grasp tightly to their shards and remember
Unwritten books of life and death begin their first chapters
The maw closes, each shard records tales never to be told

Families try to be brave and grasp their fragment of reality
In the last somber moments, a new path is now theirs
The shadow of unity fades into fear and false normality
Families divided, yet waiting for two fragmented shards of hope
For some the shards will never reunite, a daily dread

The mournful bugle announces the lost shards and moments
Moments lost in time to be remembered in another reality.

Author's Comments

Youth, a time of questioning, exploring, and finding new boundaries. The young are not afraid to ask questions we adults long ago forgotten how to ask. No exploration of purpose is complete without the fearless eyes and opinions of our future. Youth must be served.

The next series of poems take the viewpoints of our future adults.

A CHILD'S QUESTION

Dedicated to: James

Many questions posed by great scholars are yet to be answered
So it should be at the frontier of knowledge and understanding
With profound complex simplicity an eight year old poses a paradox
Is it possible to pose an idea which has no answer?
A child's mind, place of imagination and play, a thought emerges
The thought becomes a question asked with the innocence of youth

The soft voice asks, "Who is the Father of God?"
In stunned silence I stare blankly at the source of the profound
A rare moment, the beginning of a new life quest
Perhaps the curiosity of youth will discover an unseen insight
Maybe the blinding light of material desire would end the quest
Once the question is asked, a new path to truth awaits a traveler.

BORED

We are the Bored
Persistence is futile
Your mediocrity will not be combined with our own
You will be very nervous with us

We are your kids
Nagging is brutal
Your social standards will not embraced in favor of our own
You will not know what to do with us

We are the future
Ditch the whole kit and caboodle
Your wars will not be ours
You will be unrespected by us

We are the same as you
Work and walk the poodle
Your materialism will not be ignored by us
You will humor us, as did your parents

We are the Bored.

Special note: This poem was inspired by Star Trek's the Borg.

The Bored Young Person

EFFIGY OF LIFE

Tucked in the far corner of a clothes closet resides an old box

No one remembers by who or when the taped mystery capsule came to be

One Saturday morning grudging hands bring the box into the light

In the box, the first item is an odd reddish hairy object

Brown glass eyes stare blankly at the bemused beholder

The pudgy body with a benevolent smile evokes a distant memory

Forgotten yesterdays slowly become a living procession of nows

Once the animal image embodied all that was noble and trustworthy

The furry teddy for all of its age seems unchanged and ready

A soft sigh of dismissal, adult hands return the effigy to the box

Something has changed in you

What could it be?

Teddy Bear Effigy

EYES ON THE EDGE OF FOREVER

Young eyes first behold the marvel of the night sky
Strange blurry blinking lights everywhere the head can turn
Some of the distant points form shapes and names, why?
A pale rising moon no longer holds curious eyes, so much to learn
Fueled by tales of the imagination the mind breaks its earthly tie

Growing eyes intently stare through the handheld glass window
Where one light faintly blinks, now many fainter lights are revealed
Arrayed in all its glory looms the Archer's Bow
The night sky's bright afterglow hints at secrets concealed
The imagination leads the eyes to find what the stellar mystery is

Time wizened eyes marvel at the machines floating far above the head
Murky colored fuzz balls crystallize into strange shaped heavenly hues
Visiting glowing balls of gas are no longer objects of dread
Deep in the cosmos unnamed planets roam in their stellar zoos
Bold visions of where future generations will tread are alive

We are the stuff of star hearts silently beckoning us to return
Future eyes will behold the edge of the now and forever.

Looking Into Forever

REMEMBERING THE FUTURE

What could have been, the path of living regrets
In the grand matrix of the living it is second guessing choices
Silent mourning for the glowing sunrise the right path begets
The fog of decision making is the hiding place of many voices.

What should have been, the path to the grail of fairness
Stinging smoke of desire dims the vision and burns the voice of truth
Herds wander using group think, even the candle of ethics is uncouth.

What would have been, the path of interrupted journeys
The length of a life thread is unknown in this universe
Many unnecessary ends are found on ER gurneys
Some trekkers heed the Siren of Change listening to its muted verses.

What is, the right path to peace and serenity
Life is its own definition with no need to know its quantity
The journey to the future is but a short path to infinity
Remember, the future is always a faint breath from total unity.

AUTHOR'S COMMENTS

A unique personal life event present an opportunity to think about the how and why of the situation. The old cliché, "what did I do to deserve this?", is a frequent question. Perhaps, the better question should be, "What is the purpose of this event?"

The reader is invited to consider the next series of poems and ask, "What would I do in this situation?"

JUROR

You will report for service...
What did I ever do to deserve this!
No way out, time to own up to a responsibility.

Perhaps this is my lucky day...
Such a large group, no one will notice me and I will be free.
So many questions and rituals, perhaps like a salmon I failed.

Then again some salmon make it, what if...
The badged Sheppard leads his new flock away into the justice vortex.
At least I am not alone, but what does that matter at the slaughter?

The herd sits in its appointed corral, dare I look at the wolf or...
Like flies on a summer day, fact, fiction, and opinion swarm about.
As the final instructions are recited the group grows uneasy.

Time to weigh the facts or is it a gathering of the impatient...
The pieces are placed in the balance of justice, yet discord reigns.
Alone I dissent, what am I prepared to do?

Jury Box

Prison Cell Block

JOURNEY TO ASTOON

Far away in the place of recited faith
Many seek out an oasis of healing
Among the learned youth a growing wraith

Brown angels in white tend the pained throng with feeling
Magis of knowledge study each malaise seeking its defeat
Many seek out an oasis of healing

In hallways of suffering, urgency is lost in a waiting seat
A guarded door opens, an angel invites entry into the lair
Magis of knowledge study each malaise seeking its defeat

Minions of pestilence never grant what's affordable or fair
Youth and Age are equals when pains and fevers rage
A guarded door opens, an angel invites entry into the lair

Pills or a trip to surgery, all available for a proper wage
The Black Shadow silently seeks the denied or failed cure
Youth and Age are equals when pains and fever rage

What of the learned youth growing sick chasing money's lure?
Far away in the place of recited faith
The Black Shadow silently seeks the denied or failed cure
Among the learned youth a growing wraith.

Special note:

Astoon Hospital is located in Al Khobar, KSA.
This was my first visit to a foreign hospital.
Seems the problem no money/no medicine, exists worldwide.

In this poem the word wraith is defined as anger.
It is a rare use of the word.

LIGHTNING STORM ELOCUTION

Man's power has failed, Nature's power now reigns supreme,

What remains is darkness punctuated by jagged blue-white ribbons,

Loud trumpet roars signal the departure of each light ribbon,

Alone I sit watching and hearing while pondering the words of others,

Storm driven rain falls ever faster as questions pelt my mind,

Surging winds blow away present things leaving the emerging future,

Will the passing storm nurture the land or cause a disaster?

The air is charged with fear and hate, it is slowly breathed in,

The ionized air cannot conceal the fetid stench of greed and theft,

Dark clouds part revealing the face of a Hunter's Moon,

One by one the poli-pires begin their baleful howl for war blood,

Rising from my rocking chair I can see Destiny Star glittering,

The Id resonates on one important question, yet unanswered,

Am I a power of one proposing Peace or a warrior without a battle?

Summer Lightening Storm

Green Tea Under The Oak Tree

Steamy hazy days in the autumn of life

A time for slowing down and pondering the game thus far

A glass of cold honey sweetened green tea to drink while musing alone

In the shade of the oak tree each sip brings thoughts, poems, and Zen

A soothing gulp of icy green tea gives birth to a new idea

A fresh zephyr of insight allows the mind to see the crystal anew

Ice tinkling in the sweaty glass sets into motion the Zen of poetry

Does a poet happen or can it be educated to happen?

Perhaps one is born liking green tea or maybe one can drink it and...

If a poet becomes educated is it less than before?

When the ice melts the tea becomes weak and uninteresting

Live life to the fullest, strengthen it with many experiences

This is the Zen of the poet, the true path to find poetry

Green tea and poetry soothing and enlightening.

Author's Comments

Every writer has a personal favorite, in the case of the poet it is instead, personal favorites. Every so often, a work becomes a personal favorite of mine due to either its unique form or unusual theme. These poems are mostly one of a kind due to their unorthodox explorations of inner feelings or meditations.

TEARS

For Hillary Earthly (Earthman)

The Soul's eye gazes at the barren world of manliness

A waterless place imposed on me upon the death of my youth

Alone in my Island of Solitude my heart remembers the time of tears

The Mind tries to reject the feelings, but the Soul craves them!

Tears of pain, sorrow, joy, desolation, and loss; all known to me

Why is it such a terrible deed to shed tears before others?

Behind closed doors the man-mask is cast aside so the Soul may soar

Tears of joy well up as the Mind releases in emotional abandon!

With pen in hand I write my poems of Peace, Hope, and Renewal

My given words find no understanding in the barren world of no tears

Silently I read the misunderstood verse and remember what inspired it

For some unexplained reason it is now difficult to read the words

Drops of moisture appear on the paper where my words are written

Now I remember it all, these are my tears!

The tears have found unity with the Mind and Soul by using my words

Now I understand the why of the tears.

A DELICATE TIME

A nightmare can end or become a new reality,

Eyes can open to see the light, but a mind can stay closed,

Bones and muscles move to obey the hidden mind's commands,

Ideas of Peace and Tolerance come from a conscious reasoning mind,

Sudden death by unknown hands make the eyes close and body numb,

Twilight fog of fear and anger disrupt the flow of time and space,

To survive the madness the sleeper must awaken,

A new reality is a delicate time for changes in thought,

To live in the nightmare of the past or go to dreams of the future?

A choice for our times.

MUSE CATS OF THE ID

Dedicated to: The Muse Cats

In the playhouse of the Id the master performers are near,

Eagerly I await their performance with pen in hand and paper,

The stage is set with Peace, Harmony, and Tranquility,

The stage is softly lit; this is a place of infinite diversity,

Comforting, but strange fractal music resonates the Soul,

Silently the Mind Fog curtain rises up and there they are!

Muse Cats dancing, interacting with the lights, and singing to me!

All new combinations, possibilities, and bold creations for me,

Feverishly I write and fill pages knowing this moment could end,

Then suddenly as it began, all became silent in the playhouse,

The Muse Cats of The Id speak a parting soliloquy and depart,

Positive attitude leads to positive output, you can write poetry!

The Muse Cats

REFLECTIONS UPON A MIDNIGHT CANDLE

All is silent on the Isle of Solitude, it is a time of reflection,
A single lit candle stands between the Mind and the Truth,
Intently the Soul's Eye gazes into the flickering orange vortex,
Time and space lose their places as the flame dances in the Memories,
The bright wavering flame casts ever changing shadows on the Id,
Portents of the future, possibilities of things yet to come!
Be a point of light in uncertain times or go into the night quietly?
In a calm peaceful place the light of truth burns brightly,
Let us all light a Peace candle and be points of light,
May Peace return to all of us.

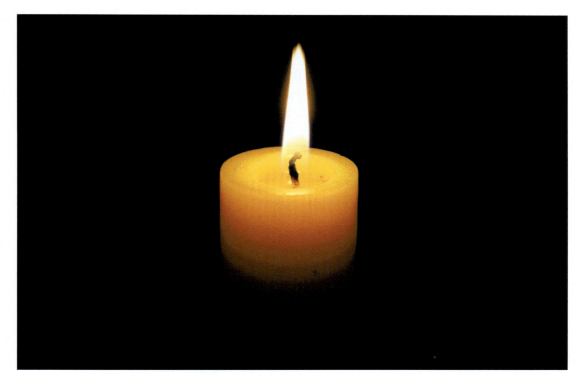

The Midnight Candle

Rough Night in Jericho

The night air is heavy with the scent of hate

lots of energy to vent

A rumble is going down tonight

someone is going to take a tumble

The Black Bone Mice

are looking for the Hissing Death Roach Camorra.

Don Bugsy gets his as the stealthy mice

drop a golf ball neat and nice

A loud CRUNCH and high bounce

the golf ball looks for another trounce

The garbage emporium of Phakrash

the Scorpion becomes the target

In the shambles of the eatery

gang leaders are swearing vendetta

Lead by the Screaming Rat Mafia

it is a street showdown for pay back

A grim scene for the Mice

the future is looking very lean

Out of a dark alley comes a thundering roar

with a wall of water

In one giant splash the entire angry scene

disappears down the gutter

Only the Spider Tong know who unleashed the deluge

Word is; Be careful how the ball bounces

or you too may be stung!

SPECIAL NOTE

'Rough Night In Jericho' is a satirical poem originally written for an assignment in the Laureate Certificate Course. The main point of the satire is to let the reader see how much like animals human street gangs are. A small mystery is contained in the poem for the reader to solve. Who turned on the water? The two clues which will give the answer are in the poem.

Camp Fire

North winds ghost through the branches of the silent witnesses
The faint breath of crystal cold quickens life to prepare
It is the time of Orion in the ascendant
Intruders into the realm of the wooden guardians seek heat and light
The glowing vortex provides comfort, it can also summon

The kingdom of the ageless giants keep many secrets
Where a mighty ancient warrior sleeps, the deepest kept secret
The invaders plunge into the heart of the leafy keep seeking pleasure
A barren circle invites the unwary to stop and stay
A lone owl warns of danger as the strangers approach

Eager hands search about for food for the roaring pyre
A collective held breath of fearful anticipation pervades
Fate is cast as the lucifer stick awakes the smoky calling flame
The unknowing gather close to the fire as the blue specter rises
Once awakened only a blood payment will quell the warrior's wrath

At gray dawn only smoking black bones remain as witness
An owl announces somberly the secret is still safe.

Special Note:

To date, this is the only poem I have written which was later converted
into a five chapter folk tale. The longer Camp Fire Story was submitted
to a short story contest four years ago.

Author's Comments

The next two poems are about Halloween (As it is known in modern times). Rarely do I write about holidays. I believe most of our holidays are excuses to run out and spend money or get acceptably drunk.

Halloween, or Samhain as it should properly be called, is the most misunderstood event to have taken place in human history. Perhaps if more were known about it, fewer would celebrate it.

SAMHAIN, SEASON OF CHANGE

Countless seasons ago in the concealed murky past is a special time
A time of harvest, a time when Orion is high in the bright cosmos
A moment of celebrating plenty and looking to tomorrows to come
An orange full moon rises above the hill, spirits and mortals gather
Spirit lamps flicker brightly with departed souls awaiting release
A silent procession of hooded priests stop at the Druid sacred mound
A blazing pyre demarks earthly light from the eternal beyond
The invocation to Salloween begins the knowing ritual
In wicker baskets hanging from log poles are the spirit possessed few
Release is now, the roaring light reaches out to touch the darkness
Each basket of screaming humanity is offered to the sacred flames
Truth Sayers arrayed about the circle intently watch the releases
In the hour of gray dawn all that remains are red glowing embers
A somber hooded line departs now knowing their destiny path
The days of Samhain are coming to an end, something new is arriving
The time of the Counterfeit Pagan will gather for Halloween instead.

A Druid Of Samhain

PAGAN TIME

Terzanelle poetic form

A moment born from the murky past
Orion is high in the clear cold earth's dome
Celebration of the new plenty, no thoughts of a winter fast

Long forgotten are the writings of the Celtic tome
No one to see the changing tomorrow in a blazing pyre
Orion is high in the clear cold earth's dome

Tales of death and fear told to youth who never tire
Concealed innocence seeking out trinkets of sweet
No one to see the changing tomorrow in a blazing pyre

No Druid priest to be found at the new pagan meet
False players and gore knocking greedily at a home's door
Concealed innocence seeking out trinkets of sweet

Very few alive to recall and tell the true all hallows lore
Destructive vile ones seek evil deeds so they can vex
False players and gore knocking greedily at a home's door

The new Pagan time without anyone to cast a nasty hex
A moment born in the murky past
Destructive vile ones seek evil deeds so they can vex
Celebration of the new plenty, no thoughts of a winter fast.

AUTHOR'S COMMENTS

The next two poems of this book express a personal viewpoint (Vortrekker) and a philosophical view point (Wyang Conclusion). The word Vortrekker comes from the Afrikaans language. It means long walker.

Vortrekker has as its inspiration the movie Blade Runner, in particular the dying soliloquy of the last android. Most poignant is the line that goes in part, "All these memories will be lost ...." I personally identify with the thought of a lifetime of experiences being lost due to disbelief.

The Wyang, shadow puppet shows telling of the struggles of good and evil from the Asian perspective. In the West, we desire a clear answer to questions and situations. Only Admiral Hyman Rickover, USN successfully developed a system to handle a situation with no right or wrong answers. The Asian mind knew of situations with no clear conclusions centuries before. The Wyang Plays teaches this to generations even today.

VORTREKKER

Oh, the myriad of sights these eyes have seen on Terra 3,

Some sorely test the mind's capacity to fathom reality from fantasy,

With the telling of each event the truth dances about like a mirage,

Such is the lot of a Vortrekker on the lifelong Mind Quest for Peace,

Each venture towards the horizon of the unknown adds understanding,

Yet understanding turns to mystery with disbelief when shared,

Each journey brings the folly of returning to tell of it,

The tell finds fewer ears when the howling winds of war roar louder,

People visualize electronic lies, believing without question,

All these treks and their stories will be lost one day soon,

The Vortrekker's last trek beyond the frontier will never be told,

The Mind Quest for Peace will continue.

WYANG CONCLUSION

"All is clouded by desire"

The ever flickering fire of life lights the screen of existence

The cosmos witnesses the Wyang play as it creates thought

Shadows of reality move and play about on the mind's eye

Light and dark silently blend to form an idea

"If it exists it is real"

An idea becomes real when acted upon

The smoke of emotion conceals the idea's true nature

Only the shadow's movement reveals light and darkness

Enlightenment or desire determines the outcome

"What then must we do?"

Add your light to the greater sum to see the Wyang unfolding

Seek balance in all things to see the shadows clearly

Life is its own answer, it needs no explanation.

The Wyang seeks no conclusion about the why of existence

Wayang Kulit

SOMETHING TO THINK ABOUT
WORDS FOR OUR TIMES

Dedicated to: Joseph Alexander

Optimism the first line of defense against depression
Victory is just one step beyond failure, take it!
Each day gives opportunity, seek it out
Reality is as it should be, flow with it,
Conquer fear by knowing and respecting yourself
Other people have feelings, never forget this
Money is a tool, not your obsession
Excite the mind with new knowledge today

Alone you are vulnerable, with friends you are strong
Do your best on a task, don't dwell on the difference
Volunteer at least once, show you are the caring one
Every person has value, never forget this
Reject intolerance, it locks you away from knowledge!
Spend time in Peaceful meditation, the soul needs it
Issues are best resolved with a rested calm mind
Teach the children in some capacity, they are the future
You must always overcome adversity with lasting Peace!

EPILOGUE

The Saudi Arabian experience continues, even though this book has come to its end. Places such has Egypt and Turkey have been visited in the recent past. Their story will be told in a future book, along with other ventures into the "Unexplored Territory". Why do I do these things? The purpose for my being resides, out there on one of those unexplored far horizons.

Desert Caravan

Printed in the United States
By Bookmasters